WRITER'S MAGAZINE
Real-Life Reading and Writing

PICTURE PERFECT

· · · · · · · · · · · · ·

BIG DREAMS

· · · · · · · · · · · · ·

WARM FRIENDS

· · · · · · · · · · · · ·

FULL SAILS

· · · · · · · · · · · · ·

ALL SMILES

Harcourt Brace & Company

Orlando Atlanta Austin Boston San Francisco Chicago Dallas New York Toronto London

WRITER'S MAGAZINE

PICTURE PERFECT   BIG DREAMS   WARM FRIENDS
FULL SAILS   ALL SMILES

CONTENTS

For permission to reprint copyrighted material, grateful acknowledgment is made to the following sources:

Felice Holman: "At the Top of My Voice" from *At the Top of My Voice and Other Poems* by Felice Holman. Text copyright © 1970 by Felice Holman. Published by Charles Scribner's Sons.

Richard Lewis: "I Love the World" by Paul Wollner from *Miracles: Poems by Children of the English-Speaking World*, edited by Richard Lewis. All rights reserved. Text © 1966 by Richard Lewis. Distributed by The Touchstone Center, New York.

National Wildlife Federation: Adapted from "Robo-Bug" by Deborah Churchman in *Ranger Rick* Magazine, October 1993. Text copyright 1993 by National Wildlife Federation. "Puffins" from *Your Big Backyard* Magazine, December, Series II. Text copyright 1981 by the National Wildlife Federation.

Tom Tucker, 421 Nevada Dr., Erie, PA 16505: Illustrations by Tom Tucker (Retitled: "Turtle Takes a Bath"). Originally published as "Critter Crack-ups" in *Ranger Rick* Magazine, March 1995.

Illustration: Bernard Adnet 72, 78-79, 85; Shirley Beckes 6-7; Paige Billin-Frye 32; Paul Borovsky 1-3, 94; Elizabeth Brandt 16; Jane Caminos 66-67, 76-77; Genevieve Claire 14-15; Roger DeMuth 8-11; Daniel Dumont 12; Rob Dunlavey 17, 28-29, 94; Patrick Girouard 33; Tim Haggerty 42-45; Maj-Britt Hagsted 50-51; Susan Hall 48-49, 62-65; Joan Holub 86; Linda Helton 24-27; N. Jo 22-23; Anne Kennedy 34-35; Bonnie Mathews 38-39; Jenny Sachs 70; Andrew Shiff 46-47; Pat Schories 68-69; Stephen Schudlich 30-31, 52, 54-55, 71, 92-93; Sharp Design 80-83; Bob Shein 72-75; Slug Signorino 36-37; Jackie Snider 28-29, 40-41; Cat Stephens 56-57; Beata Szpura 56-57; and Jackie Urbanovic 60-61.

Photography: Peter Arnold, Inc./Michael Fairchild 13*b*, Stephen J. Krasemann 53*t*, Bruno J. Zehnder 20*b.l.*; Bruce Coleman/J.C. Carton 12*b.*, Hans Reinhard 12*t.*, Dick George 18; Dwight H. Kuhn 20*t.l.&r.*, 21; Corbis/Alissa Crandall 34*l*, Staffan Widstrand 34*r.*; Photo Researchers/Francois Gohier 88, Sylvain Grandadam 91, Anthony Mercieca 52, Nuridsany et Perennov 4, Leonard Lee Rue III 5, M.H. Sharp 53*b.*, Bonnie Sue 13*t.*; Super Stock 4-5.

Creative Direction: Brian Kobberger, Stevie Pettus-Famulari/Bill SMITH STUDIO

Printed in the United States of America

1 2 3 4 5 6 7 8 9 10   030   2001 2000 99 98   ISBN 0-15-310816-9

PICTURE PERFECT

Look inside! Here's what you'll find!

_____'S
(your name)
Magazine

Signs, Signs, Everywhere!

The boy in *What I See* saw lots of things. Signs help you know what you see. They help you know what to do, too. What do these signs tell you?

Tickets

Read the signs with children, and talk about what they mean. Help them complete the blank signs. Point out the empty vendor's cart and animal area. Children can draw things in the cart and animals in their area and write signs for them.

Help the signmaker make new signs.

Keep Off the Grass

Do Not Feed the Animals

Bike Path

EXIT

Balloons

Make a sign you can use at home. Where will you put it? What will it say?

WHAT IS IT CALLED?

Real-Life LABELS Skills

A duck was one of the animals in *Down on the Farm*. You can find out about a real one.

Tail

Wing

Bill

Foot

PICTURE PERFECT — Harcourt Brace School Publishers

🍎 Read and discuss the labels with children, and have them write labels for the cat.

Label the cat with words from the box.

Eye
Nose
Ear
Leg
Tail

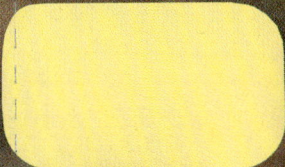

Real-Life Challenge

Draw your pet or an animal you like. Label as many parts as you can.

A Great Place to Play!

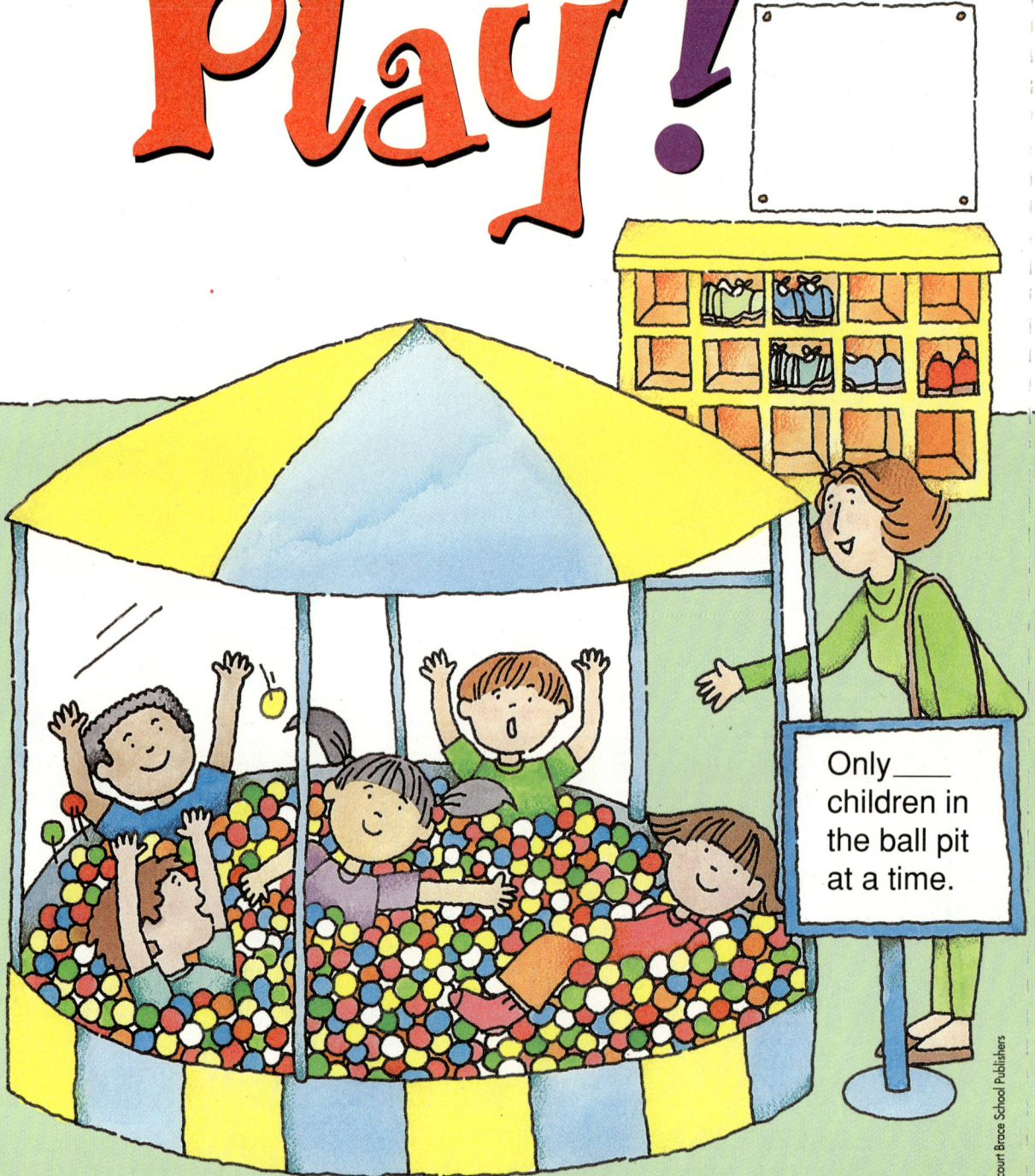

Only ____ children in the ball pit at a time.

Read the signs with children, and have them fill in the blanks or the missing information. Guide them in thinking logically about what belongs on the signs. Ask children what items the boy on page 7 can buy with his tickets.

PICTURE PERFECT — *Harcourt Brace School Publishers*

Fill in what is missing from the game signs.
Draw yourself somewhere in the picture.

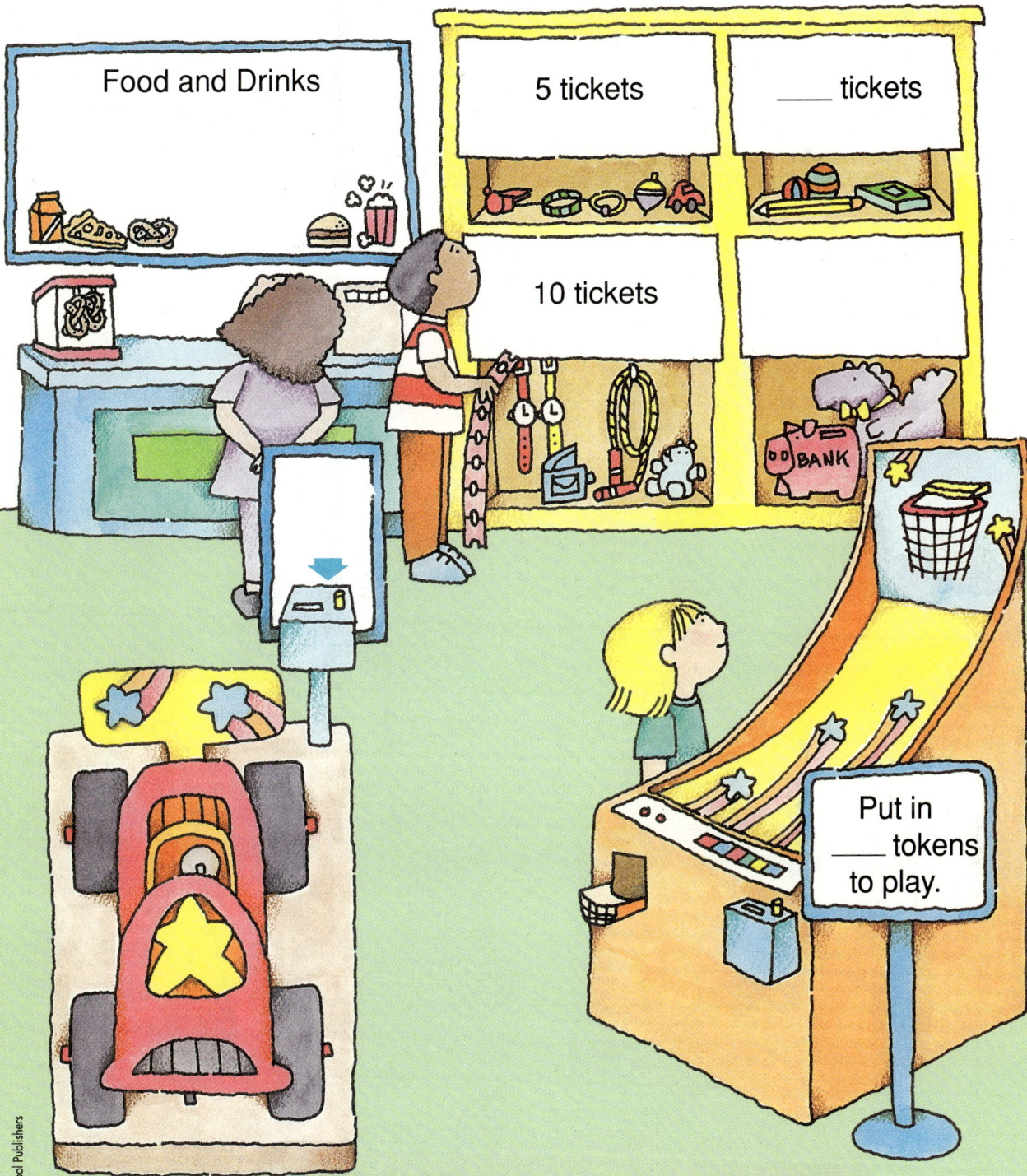

Food and Drinks

5 tickets

____ tickets

10 tickets

BANK

Put in ____ tokens to play.

Real-Life Challenge

The next time you visit a play area like this, read the signs. Help little children by reading the signs to them.

Mark That Place

Rabbits jump on a mat in *Five Little Rabbits*. Jump to the library to read more about rabbits. You might even find some bookmarks like these at the library.

Reading
Takes You
Places!

Jump
into a
Good Book!

Look for this bunny book!

Rabbits on Rollerskates by Jan Wahl

Have children pull out pages 9–10 and set them aside.

Then read and discuss the bookmarks on pages 8 and 11 with children.

Point out that the purpose of the words on bookmarks is to make people want to read.

Have children notice what is missing from some bookmarks and add to them as needed.

PICTURE PERFECT – Harcourt Brace School Publishers

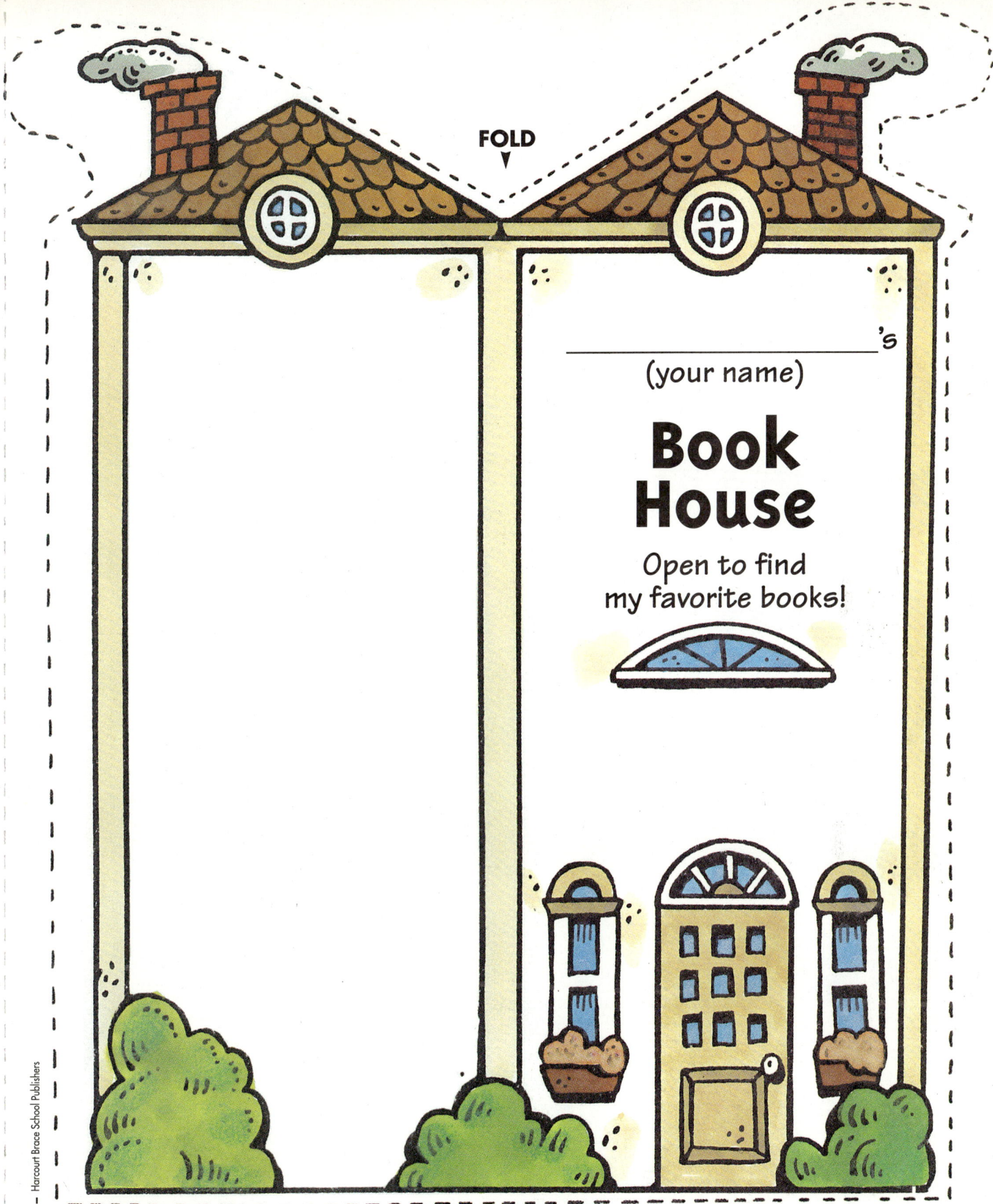

FOLD

_____'s
(your name)

Book House

Open to find
my favorite books!

PICTURE PERFECT – Harcourt Brace School Publishers

Help children assemble their bookmarks. Guide them in thinking of their own reading slogans to write on their bookmarks. Children can decorate their bookmarks and write the titles of their favorite books on the bookshelves inside.

FOLD

PICTURE PERFECT – Harcourt Brace School Publishers

I LOVE BOOKS BEARY MUCH!

♥ ♥ ♥

What's beary fun to read?
A beary good book!

What book has three bears

and a girl in it?

_____

_____

_____

Real-Life Challenge

Look for bookmarks at the library or at a
bookstore. Have a family member help you read
them. What do the bookmarks say that makes you
want to read?

Pigs and Friends

There was a pink pig in *I Went Walking*. Here are more pink pigs. Read about them under the pictures.

Large pigs like these weigh 500 pounds—or more!

Baby pigs are called piglets. A piglet weighs just over 2 pounds when it is born.

🍎 Read and discuss the captions and pictures with children. Children can write their own captions for the pictures on page 13.

PICTURE PERFECT – Harcourt Brace School Publishers

Real-Life Challenge

Look for sentences under pictures in magazines and books. Ask someone to read them with you.

Let's Go Food Shopping

Popcorn is a fun snack to eat. Here's a place where you can find popcorn.

FOOD STORE

BANANAS   ORANGES   APPLES

15

OPEN

Read the signs with children and discuss the purpose of a grocery store. On the next page, have children read the signs and draw pictures to go with them. Then have them write words for the blank signs, using the picture clues.

PICTURE PERFECT — Harcourt Brace School Publishers

What other foods can you find at a food store? Write or draw what can go on each shelf.

SNACK

FRUIT

Real-Life Challenge

The next time you visit a store, look at the signs. See if the store is like this one.

At the Top of My Voice

When I stamp
The ground thunders,
When I shout
The world rings,
When I sing
The air wonders
How I do such things.

by Felice Holman

I Love the World

I love you, Big World.
I wish I could call you
And tell you a secret:
That I love you, World.

by Paul Wollner, age 7
San Francisco, California

PICTURE PERFECT — Harcourt Brace School Publishers

BiG DREAMS

Here's what you'll find inside!

Big DREAMS — Harcourt Brace School Publishers

_____'s
(your name)
Magazine

Big, BIG News

A bear paints in *Big Brown Bear*. Here's a newspaper story about another big animal that likes to paint.

An Elephant Artist

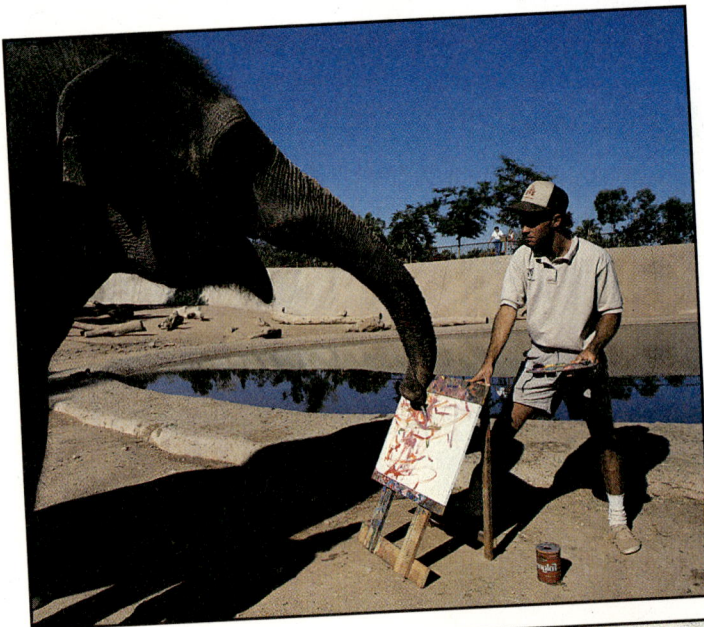

What do elephants do for fun? This elephant paints! Ruby lives in the zoo in Phoenix, Arizona. These are some of Ruby's paintings.

The zoo sells her paintings. The money helps elephants all over the world.

Read the news story to children, and discuss it with them. Then have children work with partners or in small groups to complete the activity on the next page.

BIG DREAMS — Harcourt Brace School Publishers

What is the news where you live? Write your own news story. Draw a picture to go with it.

Real-Life Challenge

Bring a news story with a picture to school. Write some sentences about the picture. Ask your teacher to read the news story to you. Were your sentences like the news story?

A PUFFIN IS A PUFFIN

You read about two kinds of birds in *The Chick and the Duckling*. Find out about another kind of bird.

This mother puffin lays one white egg in her underground home.

The puffin chick is a downy, black and white puff-ball.

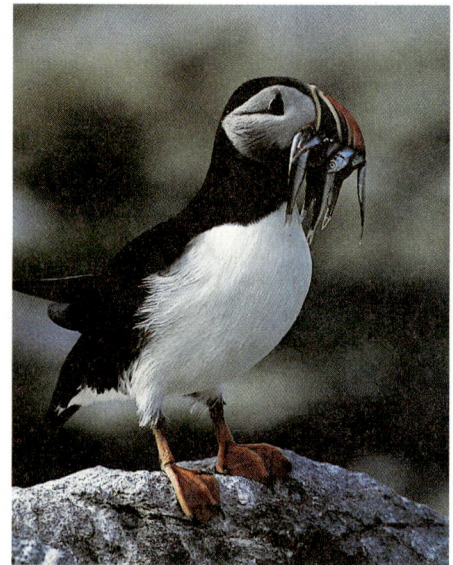

Father and mother puffin feed fish to their chick.

Read the article with children, and discuss the basic arrangement of the words near the pictures that they tell about. Point out that the words are missing from page 21. Children can help finish the article by writing some sentences that tell about the picture.

BIG DREAMS — Harcourt Brace School Publishers

Write some sentences to go with this picture.

R e a l - L i f e   C h a l l e n g e

Find a magazine article, and read it with a family member. Paste the article on a sheet of paper, and add some sentences of your own. Share your work with others.

PLANTING TIME

A sunny day is a good day for planting a garden. You might start with seed packs like these.

CARROT

Fast-Grow Seed Co.

HOW TO GROW CARROTS

1. Plant seeds 1 inch deep.

2. Water right away.

3. Do not let soil get dry.

SUNFLOWER

Fast-Grow Seed Co.

How to Grow SUNFLOWERS

1. Plant seeds 1 inch deep.

2. Plant seeds 1 foot apart.

3. Water every week.

Help children read and discuss the seed packages. Then have them make the front and back of their own seed package.

BIG DREAMS – Harcourt Brace School Publishers

What will you plant? Make up your own seed pack for a vegetable or a flower. Use words and pictures on your seed pack.

Fast-Grow Seed Co.

Radish

Lettuce

Tomato

Pansy

Green Bean

Daisy

Real-Life Challenge

Look for seed packs in a store or garden center. Look at the pictures, and read the words with a family member. See if the seed packs look like the one you made.

ON THE

In *Moving Day*, a big truck helped the Kims move. What do these trucks do? How can you tell?

READY RECYCLING

REDUCE → **REUSE** → **RECYCLE**

Flora's Flowers

Lunch on the Go

BIG DREAMS — Harcourt Brace School Publishers

Read the signs with children, and discuss the purpose of each vehicle. Help children recognize the clues for the uses of the vehicles.

MOVE

Pizza to You

Betty's Bikes

CITY CEMENT

Write words to go on each truck or van. Add pictures and color them, too.

Have children make up their own uses for the plain vehicles and make their own signs. Encourage children to make one of the vehicles a moving truck.

Real-Life Challenge

Look for trucks and vans in your neighborhood. Write and draw what you see on them.

GREAT WORK!

In *Catch Me If You Can,* a little dinosaur thought her grandpa was great! Maybe she even gave him an award. Here's another kind of award.

GOOD JOB

Elton Roberts

You have won the

HAPPY HELPER AWARD

for

✔ helping others with their work.
✔ helping the teacher.
✔ helping with a smile.

Thank you,
Your Teacher

Read and discuss the award with children. Brainstorm a list of school workers, family members, and others who do something special. Each child can choose someone to make an award for on page 29.

BIG DREAMS — Harcourt Brace School Publishers

Make a special award for someone you know.

Real-Life Challenge

Look for awards hanging in your school. Look for them on books and in restaurants. Find out what they say.

ToYS FOR YOU!

Andy wanted someone to play with in *Later, Rover*.
Maybe he would like to play with the dog in this ad.

EVERYONE Wants
REMMY
the Remote-Control Dog

A Kid's Best Friend

Sits and Shakes Hands

BIG DREAMS — Harcourt Brace School Publishers

Read the advertisement with children. Invite them to comment on the design elements that make the ad look inviting. Have children make their own ad on page 31.

Write your own ad!

Real-Life Challenge

Cut out two magazine ads—one that you like and one that you don't like. Bring them to share in class. Tell what you like about your favorite ad. Tell what you do not like about the other ad.

These six pictures are hidden on the page. Find the pictures and circle them.

WARM FRIENDS

What will you find in this part of your magazine? Take a look!

WARM FRIENDS – Harcourt Brace School Publishers

_____'s
(your name)
Magazine

Which Is Which?

What kind of fox did Hattie see? These labels show the differences.

little ears

big ears

long nose

short nose

red fur

Red Fox

white fur

Arctic Fox

🍎 Help children read the labels and compare the two kinds of foxes. Then guide children in comparing the dogs on the next page. Have them work with partners to write the labels.

WARM FRIENDS — Harcourt Brace School Publishers

How are these two dogs different?
Write labels with words from the box.

long legs
short ears
long tail
long ears

Real-Life Challenge

Find pictures of two animals you like. Show them to a friend or a family member. Then talk about how the animals are different.

FUNNY FRIENDS

Real-Life CARTOONS Skills

Stanley wanted to be the little girl's friend.
Read this cartoon about two friends.

Why do you always know what time it is?

Didn't you know? I'm a watch dog!

Help children read the cartoon on this page. Have them talk about the cartoon on the next page and suggest what the two characters might be saying. Then have children write one or two sentences in the speech balloons.

Here's another cartoon.
Add your own sentences.

Look for other cartoons.
Share them with a friend.

It's for You!

A boy tells his uncle all about his friends in "Best of Friends." Sometimes friends give each other gifts. The tag tells who gave the gift.

For Jay
I miss you!
Love, Grandma

Get Well Soon

To Keesha
FROM Reggie

HAPPY BIRTHDAY!

TO Sam
FROM Kari

Read the tags with children. Help them discuss what kinds of gifts have tags and what information gift tags include. Then have children write and decorate their own tags on the next page.

WARM FRIENDS — Harcourt Brace School Publishers

Now make your own gift tags.

Real-Life Challenge

Next time you get a gift, read the tag out loud.

Count Them Up

More and more animals came to live in the Shoe Town. How many animals live in this barn?

Mice	🐭 🐭 🐭 🐭
Pigs	🐷 🐷
Sheep	🐑 🐑 🐑 🐑 🐑
Cows	🐄 🐄 🐄
Hens	🐔 🐔 🐔 🐔
Horses	🐴 🐴

With children, read each graph heading. Have children count the animals in each section of the graph. Then help them count the number of girls and the number of boys in the class, and have them fill in the pictograph on the next page.

WARM FRIENDS – Harcourt Brace School Publishers

How many girls and boys are in your class? Make your own graph.

My Class

Girls	
Boys	

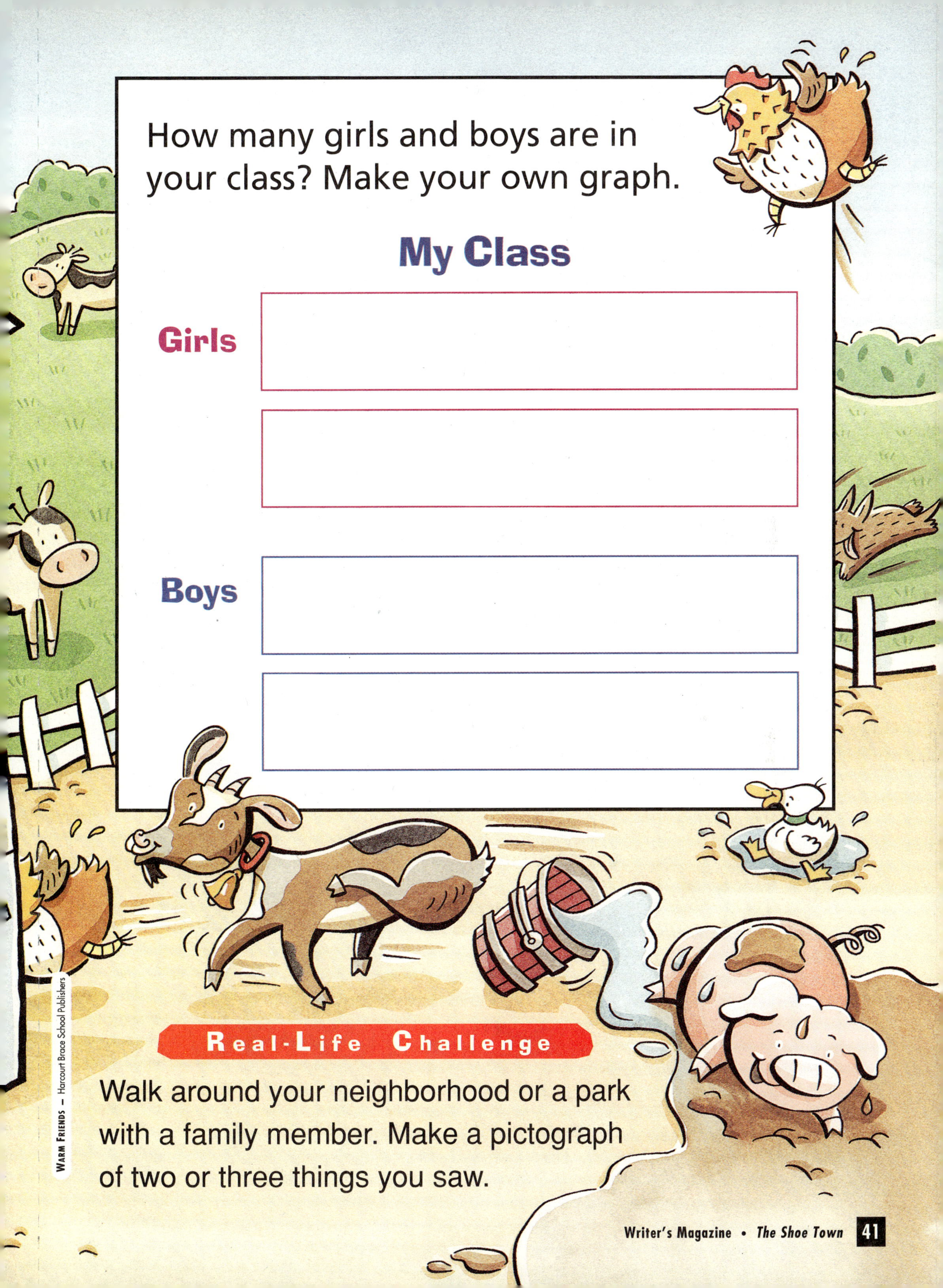

Real-Life Challenge

Walk around your neighborhood or a park with a family member. Make a pictograph of two or three things you saw.

WARM FRIENDS – Harcourt Brace School Publishers

A FREE GIFT

Friends do things together. You and a friend might have fun with lion and mouse finger puppets. Read the cereal box to find out how to get them—free!

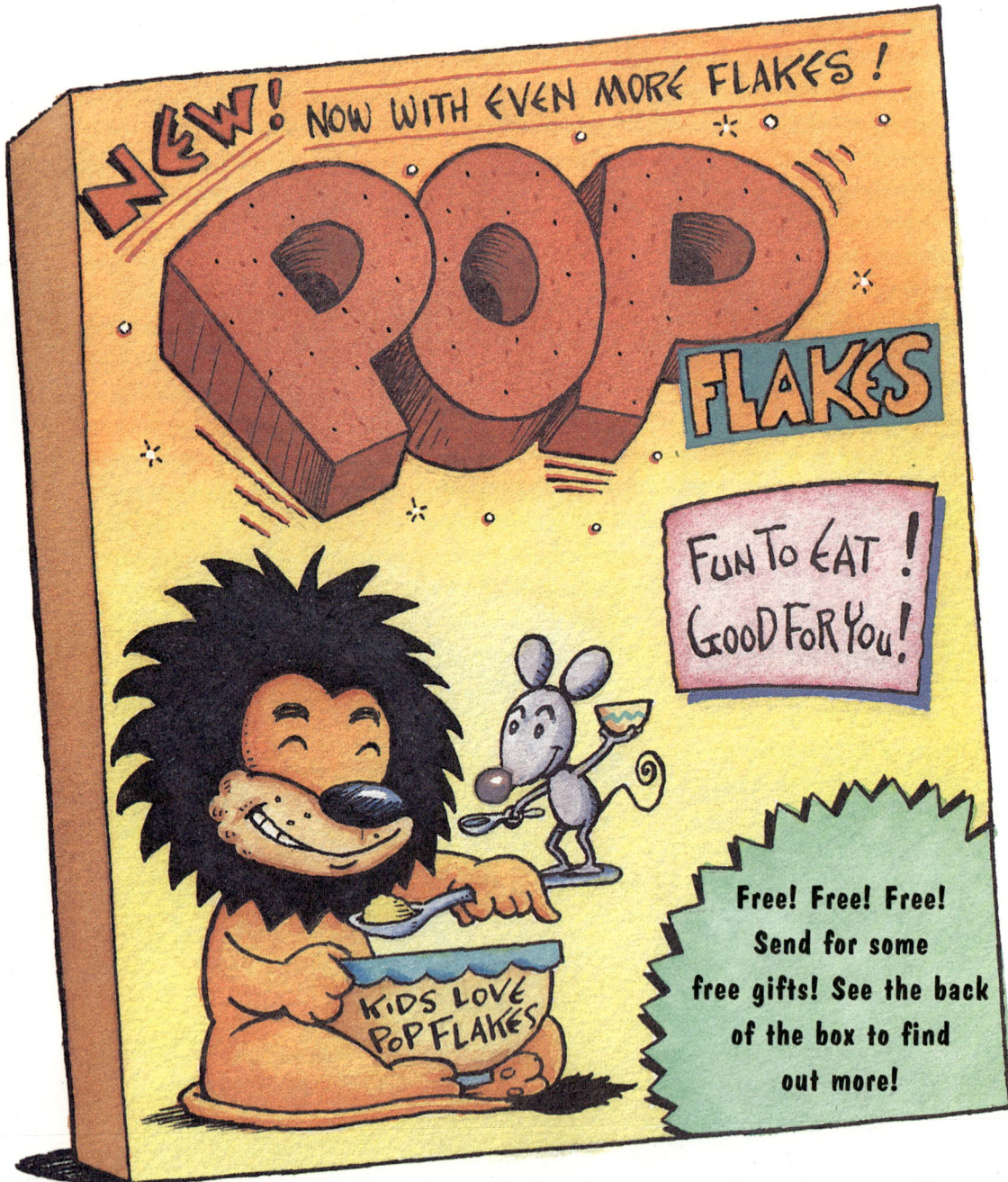

NEW! NOW WITH EVEN MORE FLAKES!

POP FLAKES

FUN TO EAT! GOOD FOR YOU!

KIDS LOVE POP FLAKES

Free! Free! Free! Send for some free gifts! See the back of the box to find out more!

WARM FRIENDS — Harcourt Brace School Publishers

Have children pull out pages 43-44 and set them aside. Read the cereal box with children. Ask them if the free gift is inside the box or if they have to send for it. Ask children what phrases might make someone want to buy the cereal. Then help them complete the form on page 45.

FOLD ▾   FOLD ▾

LION
HOUSE

FOLD ▾   FOLD ▾

MOUSE
HOUSE

1. 2. 3.

tape

Tell children to imagine that this is their free gift which has just arrived from Pop Flakes cereal. Help them assemble their finger puppets and houses. Invite them to work with a partner to plan a puppet show to share with the group.

WARM FRIENDS – Harcourt Brace School Publishers

Fill out the form to get your **free** gift!

A free gift from Pop Flakes just for YOU!

Send for the lion and mouse finger puppets. They come with houses, too! Just fill out the form. Save three UPCs from Pop Flakes boxes. Mail them with the form to get your free gift.

Please send me my free gift! I am sending 3 UPCs.

Name _____

Address _____

City_____ State_____

ZIP Code _____

Real-Life Challenge

Look at cereal boxes at home and in the store. Which ones show free gifts? Read to see if the gift is in the box or if you must send for it.

WARM FRIENDS – Harcourt Brace School Publishers

SHOW TIME!

In "Let's Dance," Rex learns how to dance. These posters tell about a special dance show.

DANCE DANCE DANCE

Come to our dance show!

Saturday at noon in Town Hall

FREE

Everyone Is Invited to Our Dance Show

Saturday — 12:00 noon
Town Hall

WARM FRIENDS — Harcourt Brace School Publishers

🍎 Help children read both posters and discuss the information they give. Then have children write and decorate their own posters on the next page.

What is happening in your school or neighborhood? Make a poster to tell people about it.

Real-Life Challenge

Look for posters near your house. Read them to someone in your family.

Here are some things friends like to do together.

Friends tell jokes.

Knock, knock.

Who's there?

Boo.

Boo, who?

Sorry that I made you cry!

Friends play games.

Miss Mary Mack — Mack — Mack
All dressed in black — black — black
With silver buttons — buttons — buttons
All down her back — back — back.

What do you like to do with your friends?

FULL SAILS

What's next in your magazine? Read this list to find out.

FULL SAILS – Harcourt Brace School Publishers

FINISH

Let's Eat!

The Little Red Hen and all her chicks ate their bread. You can choose from this menu. What would you like to eat?

Food

Best-Ever Burger $1.50

Pop's Pizza $1.25

Grilled Cheese Sandwich .... 95¢

Fresh Fruit .... 75¢

Drinks

Cold Milk .... 30¢

Hot Chocolate .... 45¢

Orange Juice .... 85¢

Read the menu with children. Have them work with partners or in small groups as restaurant servers. They can write their orders on the order pad on page 51. Discuss the usefulness of the menu and the order pad formats to give and record information. You may wish to help children use calculators to add the totals on the order form.

Full Skills – Harcourt Brace School Publishers

Pretend that you are a server. Write
on the order form what someone wants to eat.

Funtime Restaurant

May I take your order?

Food or Drink	How Many?	$ Price

Real-Life Challenge

The next time you go out to eat, look at the
menu. Read it with a family member. Maybe
you can order your own food and drink!

FULL SAILS – Harcourt Brace School Publishers

Birds, Birds, Birds

Henny Penny is a chicken. Here is a magazine article about some other kinds of birds.

All birds have feathers. All birds have wings. All birds have beaks. But not all birds look alike.

The yellow bird is a **warbler**. There are many different kinds of warblers.

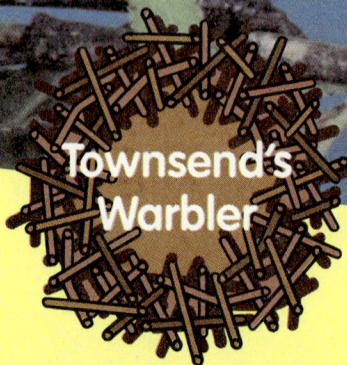

Townsend's Warbler

🍎 Read and discuss the article with children.

Cardinal

The red bird is a **cardinal**. Cardinals live in many places. They sing a cheery song.

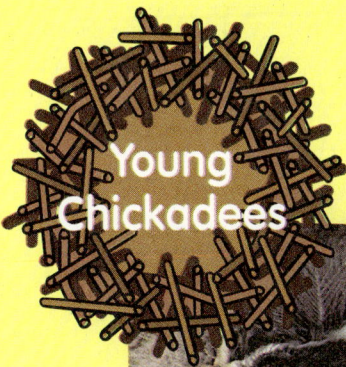

The three fluffy little birds are young **chickadees**. Maybe you have seen chickadees in your backyard.

Young Chickadees

Now turn the page and draw your very own bird!

Follow These Steps

to draw a bird of your own

1. Draw a circle for the bird's head.

2. Draw a bigger circle for the bird's body.

3. Draw a V for the bird's beak.

4. Draw eyes above the beak.

5. Draw two wings.

6. Draw two legs and little feet. Color your bird.

Read the directions with children, and have them draw their bird on page 55. Discuss the logic of numbering the directions and placing them in order. Discuss why it is important to follow each step in order.

Full Sails — Harcourt Brace School Publishers

FULL SAILS — Harcourt Brace School Publishers

Real-Life Challenge

Draw your own animal. Then write directions
that your classmates can use to draw an animal
like yours. Draw a picture to go with each step.

Sign Here

Little Lumpty did just what his mother told him not to do. Maybe he needs a contract like this one!

MY CONTRACT FOR THIS WEEK

Date _____ March 7–11 _____

My goal is to ___ stay off the wall. ___

I will ___ play safely every day. ___

I will get ___ a sticker. ___

I agree to this contract.

LUMPTY
_____

Mrs. Lumpty
_____

Monday	Tuesday	Wednesday	Thursday	Friday
Great!	Great Job!	Well Done!	☆	◯

🍎 Read and discuss with children Lumpty's contract. Talk about the purpose of a contract as an agreement. Have children think of an improvement they would like to make and have them write their own contract on the next page.

Would you like to make a contract with your teacher, a family member, or a classmate? Write your own contract.

MY CONTRACT FOR THIS WEEK

Date _____

My goal is to _____

I will _____

I will get _____

I agree to this contract.

_____

_____

Monday	Tuesday	Wednesday	Thursday	Friday

Real-Life Challenge

Your school was built by some workers. Do you think they signed a contract? What might have been written on it?

Superstar Sandwich

When Jess and her Grandad went into the woods, they took sandwiches. Maybe they made Superstar Sandwiches with this recipe.

Superstar Sandwich

Things You Need:

- star-shaped cookie cutter
- 2 slices of bread
- knife
- peanut butter
- raisins

How to Make It:

1. Cut two stars out of the bread.

2. Spread peanut butter on each star.

3. Put raisins on the peanut butter.

4. Put the star sandwich together.

Read the recipe with children. You may wish to make the sandwiches as a class activity, using various shaped cookie cutters. Discuss the format of the recipe and why it is important to list all the ingredients. Have children write their own recipes on page 59.

FULL SAILS — Harcourt Brace School Publishers

SANDWICH FOR A SQUIRREL

Write a sandwich recipe for a squirrel.
Put in things you think a squirrel would like.

Things You Need:

· ·

How to Make It:

Real-Life Challenge

Look at recipe books at home and in the library. Share them with classmates.

Thanks A Lot

Worms do so much for us! Here's a note to thank them.

Dear Wonderful Worms,

Thank you for helping me take care of my garden. You do a good job of making the soil soft and airy. Now the roots of my plants can breathe and grow.

You are a big help!

Your friend,
Sam

Read the thank-you note with children. Discuss why it is polite to write thank-you notes when people do things for you. Have children write their own thank-you notes on page 61.

Draw inside the box a gift you would like to give to Worble the Worm. Then pretend you are Worble. Write a thank-you note.

Dear _____,

Thank you for _____

_____

_____

_____

_____

_____

Your friend,

Worble

Real-Life Challenge

Think about a friend, classmate, or family member who has done something nice for you. Write a thank-you note to that person.

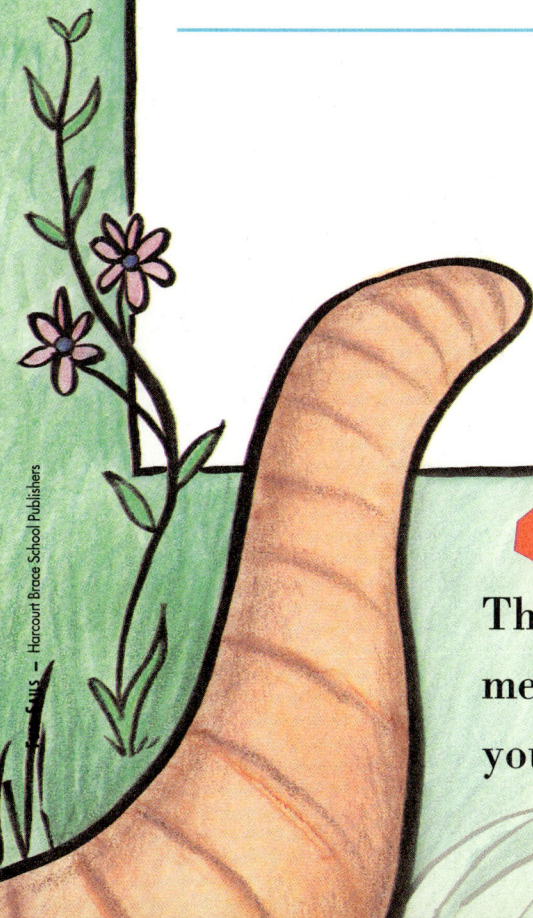

Fun and Games

Do you think Frog and Toad would like to play this game? Read the directions.

1. Cut out the frogs and cards.
2. Each player puts a frog by START.
3. Toss a coin. If you get heads, move 1 space. If you get tails, move 2 spaces.
4. If you land on the stoplight, take a card. Do what the card says to do.
5. The first one to reach FINISH wins.

START

Have children pull out page 63–64 and set it aside. Help them read the game directions. Discuss why it's important to read directions before playing a game.

FULL SAILS – Harcourt Brace School Publishers

A train is coming!

Go back **2** spaces.

The sun is shining.

Jump ahead **3** spaces.

Have children fill in their own messages on the blank game cards and draw art to correspond to their messages along the gameboard path.

FULL SAILS – Harcourt Brace School Publishers

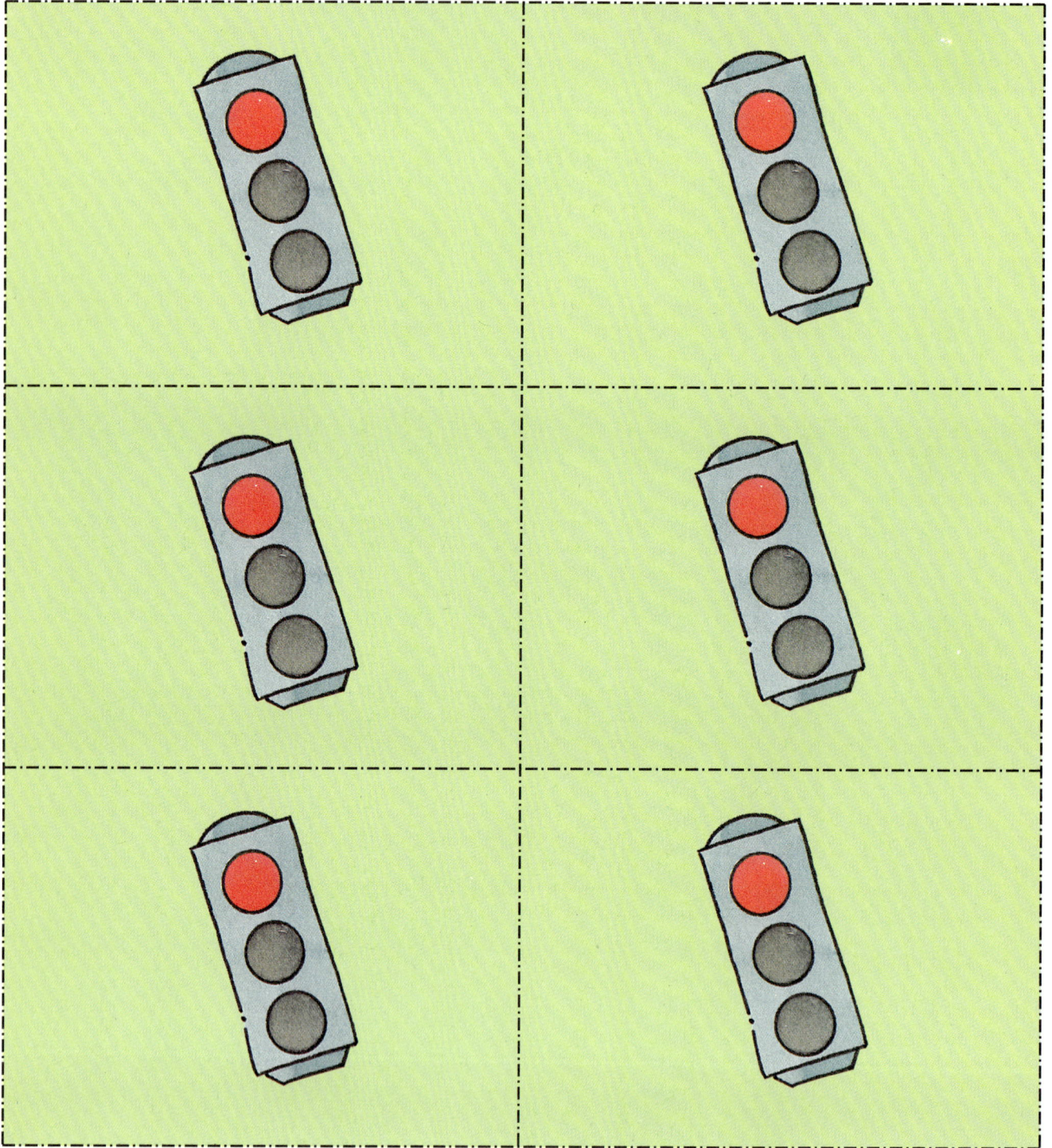

FULL SAILS — Harcourt Brace School Publishers

Real-Life Challenge

Bring a game to school.
Work with a group to read the
directions and play the game.

Whose Footprints?

Lionel and Jeffrey played in the snow.
Do you think they saw any animal tracks
there? What animals made these tracks?
Use the Map Key to find out.

MAP KEY

rabbit

fox

skunk

Help children read the map key and identify the animal that made each footprint trail. Have
them select an animal footprint from page 67 and draw and label it on the map key. Then have
children draw a path of those footprints on the map and record their observations on the chart.

FULL SKILLS — Harcourt Brace School Publishers

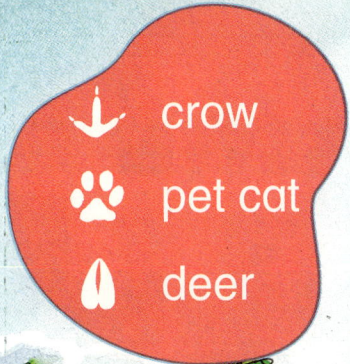

Choose an animal footprint.
Draw a path of the footprints on
the map. Then fill in the chart.

ANIMAL TRACKING CHART

Animal	Where Tracks Began	Where Tracks Ended

Real-Life Challenge

Find a map at home, or look in the
library for a book with maps. Look
at the map keys. What do they tell
you about the maps?

An Island

JENNY TOOK A PRETEND BOAT TRIP. THIS BEAR AND FOX ARE TAKING ONE, TOO. FINISH THE COMIC TO SHOW WHAT HAPPENS.

1

Look! Let's go over there! It looks like fun!

3

Have children read the beginning of the comic strip. Ask them to think of their own ending. Have children draw what happens in frames 3 and 4 and include speech balloons.

ADVENTURE

Cut out your favorite comic strips. Put them in the Reading Center for everyone to share.

Help the bird find its way to the fair.

FOOD

TICKETS

FULL SAILS — Harcourt Brace School Publishers

ALL SMILES

Look inside! Here's what you'll find!

_____'s
(your name)
Magazine

A Mouse Song

If Roberto wrote a song about his paper mouse, it might go like this.

My mouse   saved   the   cat!

My mouse   saved   the   cat!   Its

sha–dow scared   the   dog   a–way.

My   mouse   saved   the   cat!

Sing the lyrics with children to the tune of "The Farmer in the Dell." Help children pull out and assemble their songbooks. Have children recall some events from "Dreams" about which more verses could be written. Children can use the musical webs to plan more verses. Have them write their verses in the songbook and share them in small groups.

ALL SMILES — Harcourt Brace School Publishers

_____'s Songbook

Verses are sung to the tune of
"The Farmer in the Dell."

ALL SMILES — Harcourt Brace School Publishers

Use the web to plan another verse for the song. Write your new verse in your songbook.

Real-Life Challenge

Think of a special day that is coming up. Write lyrics about the special day. Sing them to a tune that you know. Then share your song.

Turtle Takes a Bath

You read about Mudge's bath. Now see what happens when Turtle takes a bath.

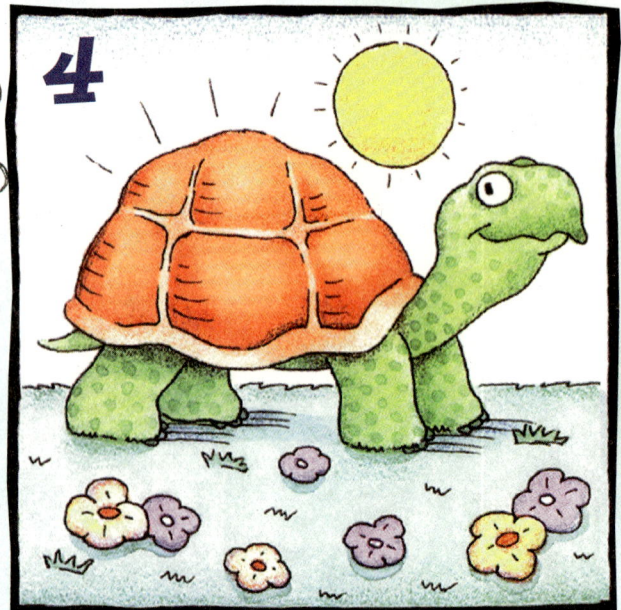

Write about what happens in "Turtle Takes a Bath." Tell the story in order.

1

2

3

4

Real-Life Challenge

Draw your own comic strip.
Write a story to go with it.

PET WEEK AT THE LIBRARY

A good place to find out more about pets is at the library. It's Pet Week at this library. Read the library announcements to find out what you can see and do.

Animals at the Library

Mrs. Roberts will bring some birds, snakes, and spiders from the zoo. They will be here at 4:00 on Monday and Wednesday.

STORIES About PETS

Listen to some funny pet stories! Story times are Tuesday and Thursday at 2:00.

MOVIE HOUR

WHEN?
Friday at 3:00

WHERE?
In the Movie Room

WHAT MOVIE?
Puff the Perfect Pet

PET CRAFTS

Make pets out of pine cones! We will meet Monday and Thursday at 1:00.

Read the announcements with children and have them write the events on the calendar.

Write on your calendar what will happen at the library.

MONDAY

TUESDAY

WEDNESDAY

THURSDAY

FRIDAY

Real-Life Challenge

Read announcements around your school and library. Write down the things you would like to see or tell your family about.

GETTING AROUND TOWN

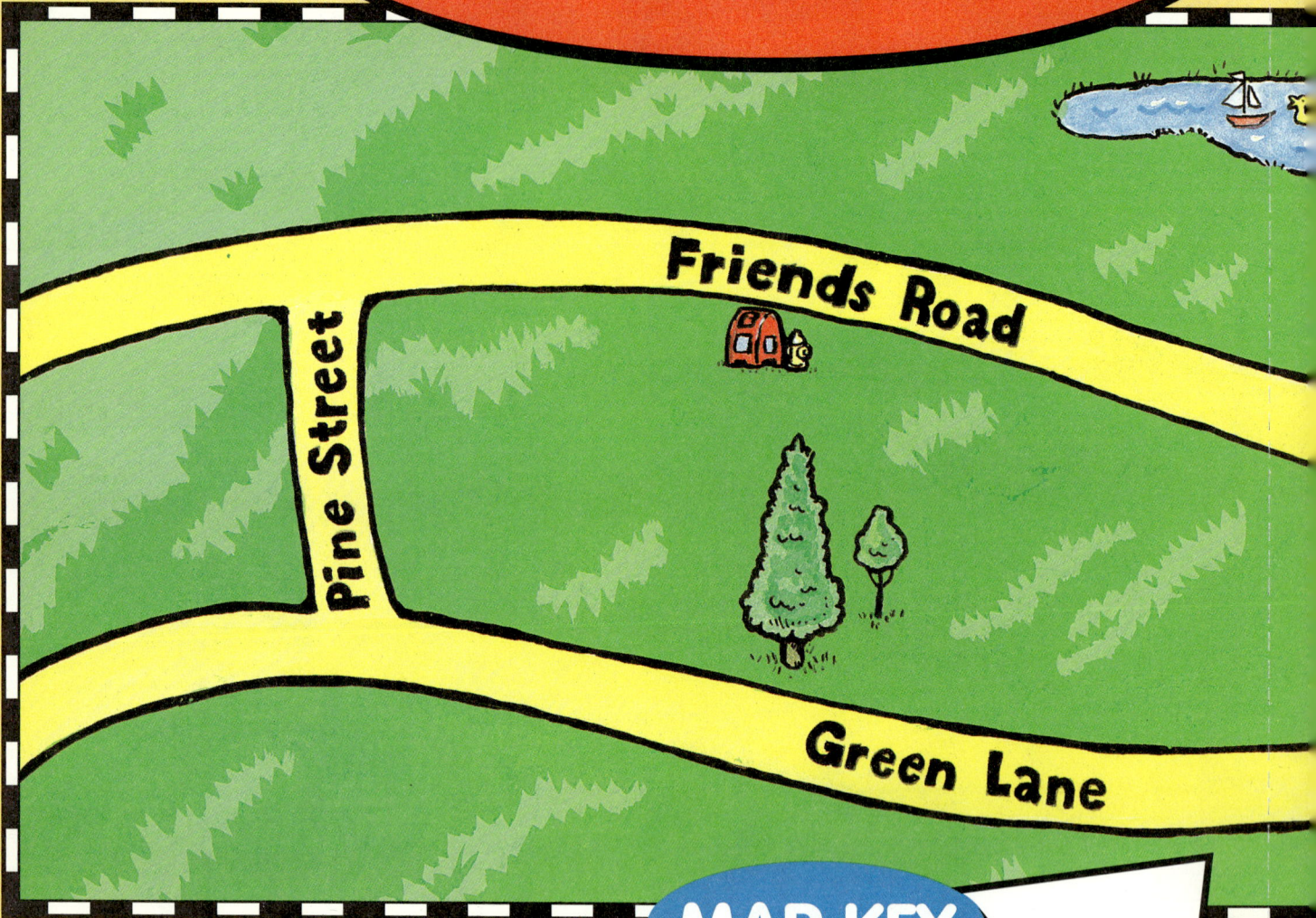

Friends Road

Pine Street

Green Lane

Edie is new in town. Make her a map to help her find her way around.

MAP KEY

House

School

Road

Playground

Store

Library

ALL SMILES – Harcourt Brace School Publishers

Have children pull out pages 81 and 82. Then read the road names and map key with children. Have them cut out the items and paste them on the map. Children can draw and cut out Edie and give her a tour of the town. Then have them work with a partner to give Edie directions to places in town.

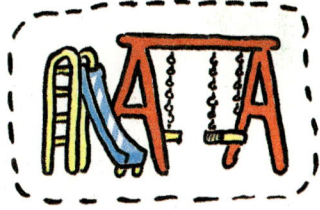

ALL SMILES – Harcourt Brace School Publishers

DIRECTIONS FOR EDIE

1 Write Edie's and Snail's name on their houses.

2 Tell Edie how to get from her house to Snail's house.

3 Tell Edie how to get from the school to the library.

4 How can she get from Snail's house to the playground?

5 Pretend you are Edie. Ask more questions about how to get around.

Real-Life Challenge

Work with a partner to draw a map of your school. Make a map key for your map.

ROBO-BUG

Read about a robot that might visit other planets someday.

Meet Hannibal, the robot ant! Hannibal has six robot legs so that it can walk like a real ant.

What can people do with a robot that is like an ant? Ants can walk very well on bumpy ground. So a robot like Hannibal would be good to send to Mars. The ground there is super bumpy!

Hannibal is about the size of a big book. Some robots will be as small as real ants. Doctors will use them to help fix small body parts like eyes.

Little robots can do big jobs!

Read the article with children, and discuss what Hannibal might someday do on Mars. Then have children read the caption for the first make-believe photograph, write their own caption for the second one, and then draw the third one and write a caption for it.

ALL SMILES – Harcourt Brace School Publishers

When Hannibal goes to Mars, the photos it takes might look like these. Draw your own picture of Hannibal on Mars. Then write captions.

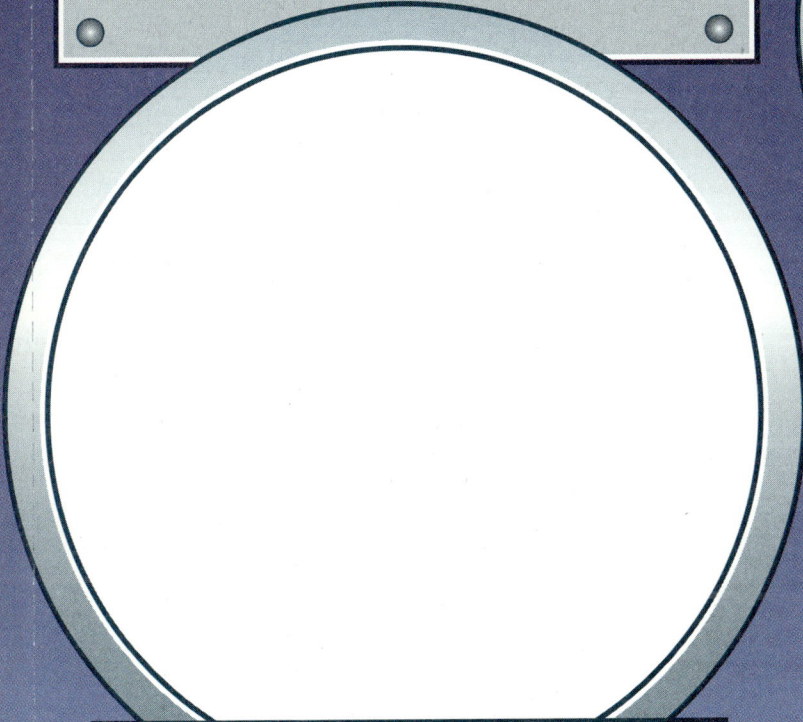

Real-Life Challenge

Get a photograph or a magazine picture. Write a caption to go with it.

TAKE A MESSAGE

Real-Life TELEPHONE MESSAGE Skills

Geraldine found out that there is more fun and more work with a new baby. One way to help is to answer the phone and take messages. Listen! The phone is ringing right now!

1

Hello. Mica speaking.

Saturday APRIL 4

2

Hi, Mica! It's Grandma. Please tell your mother that I'll bring the cake to your brother's birthday party.

3

OK, Grandma. I'll tell her. See you at the party! Good-bye!

Saturday APRIL 4

4

Good-bye!

Read the telephone conversation with children. Then invite two children to act it out. Have children refer to the telephone conversation, the calendar, and the clock to complete the message form.

Help Mica take a telephone message by filling out the form.

Message for

_____

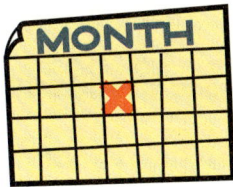 **Date**    **Time**

_____   _____

Message

_____

_____

_____

_____

_____

Alaska

In the story, you read that Julius is an Alaskan pig. Now you can read this article to learn about Alaska.

Alaska is the largest state in the United States. It is very cold there in the winter. It snows a lot. There are many beautiful things to see in Alaska. What would you like to see there?

Have children tear out pages 89 and 90. Then read the article on pages 88 and 91 with them.

Draw a picture about Alaska on the front of your postcard.

Greetings from Alaska

Ask children to imagine they are visiting Alaska. Have them make a postcard for a friend. They can write a real or made-up address on the postcard.

Write a note to a friend on the left side of your postcard.
Write a real or made-up address on the right.

ALASKA,
land of beauty

USA

Does the sun shine at midnight where you live? It does in Alaska. During the summer it is day for about three months. During the winter it is night for about three months.

Sometimes at night, beautiful lights shine in the sky. They are called the northern lights.

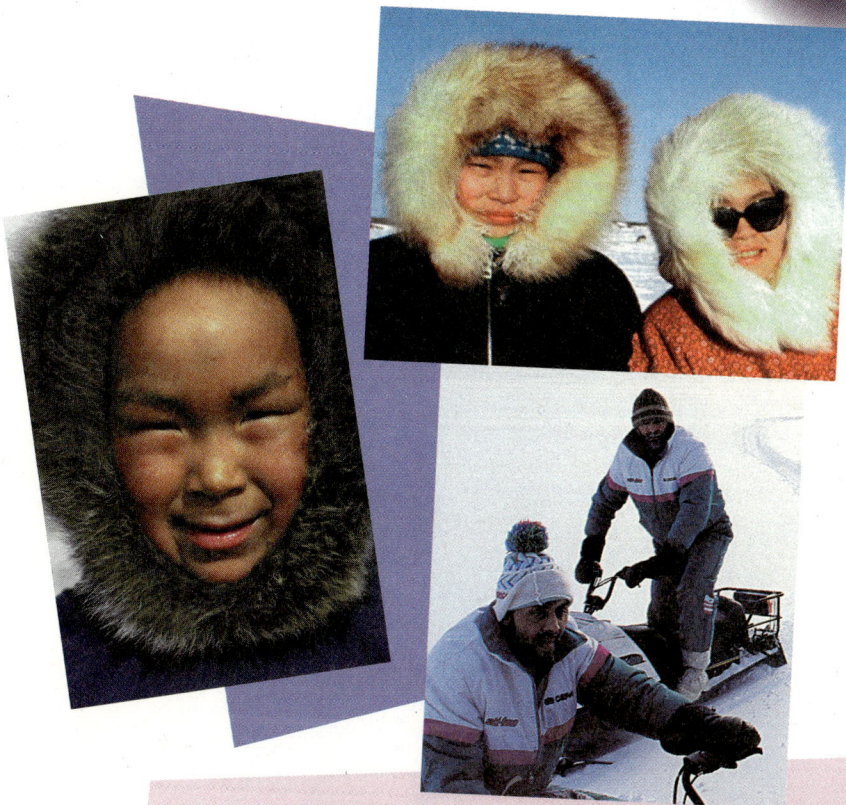

The people who live in Alaska are very proud of their state. Many people like to visit Alaska. It is a beautiful land to see.

Real-Life Challenge

Write about the place where you live or a place you would like to visit. Draw a picture to go with it. Put your sentences and picture in a class travel book.

THE FOOD PYRAMID

Silvia must have been eating right to grow into her shoes. This food pyramid shows how much you should eat from each food group every day.

Fats, Oils, and Sweets Group, only a little.

Meat, Poultry, Fish, Dry Beans, Eggs, and Nuts Group, 2–3 servings

Milk, Yogurt, and Cheese Group, 2–3 servings

Fruit Group, 2–4 servings

Vegetable Group, 3–5 servings

Bread, Cereal, Rice, and Pasta Group, 6–11 servings

OATS

Read the food pyramid with children. Discuss the usefulness of the pyramid shape as a chart. Have children use the blank pyramid to show how often they play with certain toys, showing the toys they use least at the top and those they use most at the bottom. Tell children they can show information about something other than toys if they wish.

ALL SMILES – Harcourt Brace School Publishers

Use the pyramid chart to show how much you play with each of your toys. Where should you show the toys you play with the most? Where should you show the ones you do not play with very much?

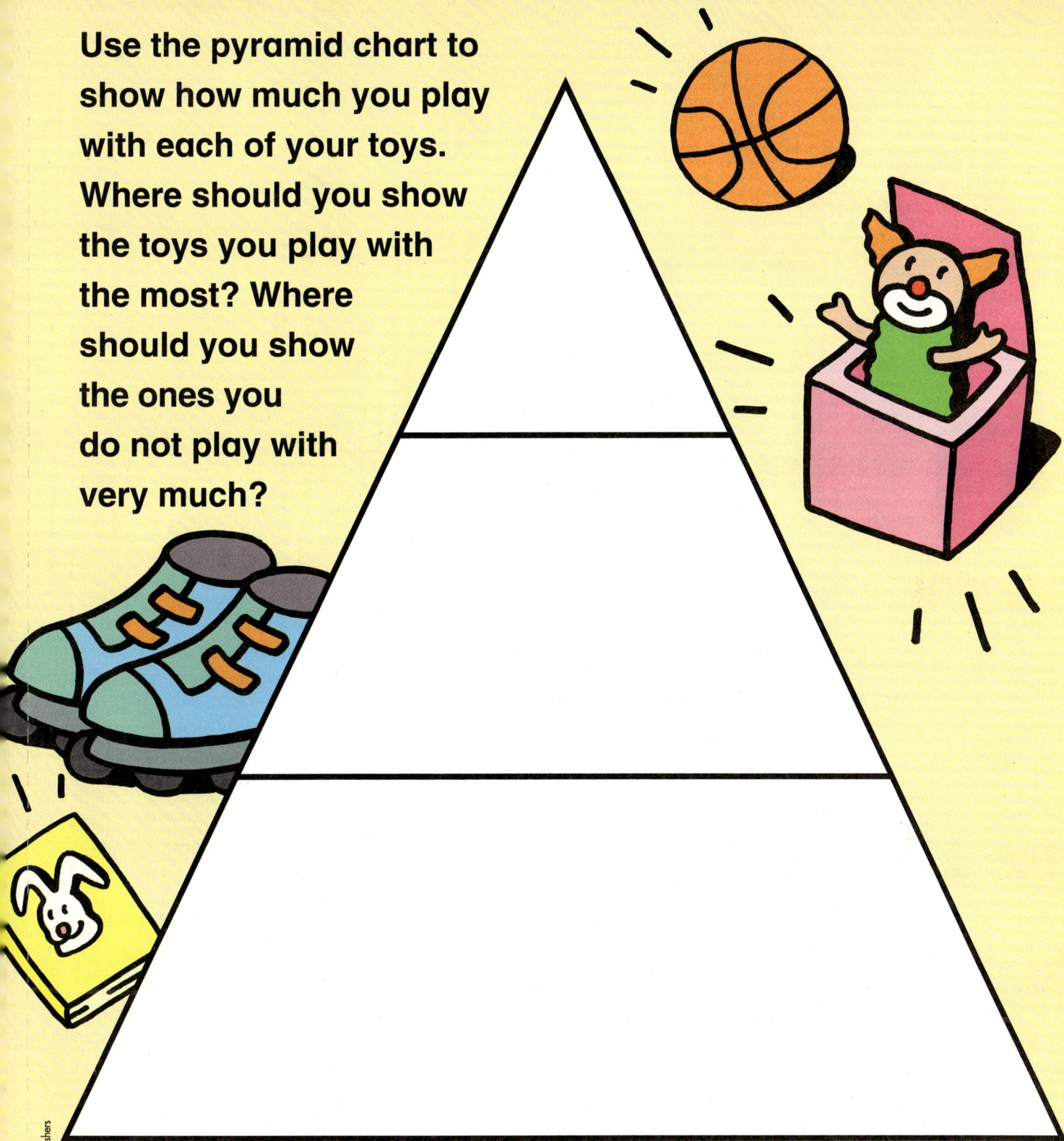

Real-Life Challenge

Draw another pyramid. Use it to show the sports you play, the foods you eat, or the books you read.

What Is Wrong?

Circle all the things that are wrong with this picture.